PEOPLE to KNOW TODAY

Sam Walton
Business Genius of Wal-Mart

By Sally Lee

Enslow Publishers, Inc.
40 Industrial Road
Box 398
Berkeley Heights, NJ 07922
USA

http://www.enslow.com

Library of Congress Cataloging-in-Publication Data

Lee, Sally.
  Sam Walton : business genius of Wal-Mart / by Sally Lee.
      p. cm. — (People to know today)
  Includes bibliographical references and index.
  ISBN-13: 978-0-7660-2692-6
  ISBN-10: 0-7660-2692-2
  1. Walton, Sam, 1918—Juvenile literature. 2. Wal-Mart (Firm)—History—Juvenile literature.
  3. Businesspeople—United States—Biography—Juvenile literature. 4. Millionaires—United States—
Biography—Juvenile literature. 5. Discount houses (Retail trade)—United States—History—Juvenile
literature. I. Title.
  HC102.5.W35L44 2007
  381'.149092—dc22
  [B]

                                2006034046
Printed in the United States of America

10 9 8 7 6 5 4 3 2 1

To Our Readers: We have done our best to make sure all Internet addresses in this book were active and appropriate when we went to press. However, the author and publisher have no control over and assume no liability for the material available on those Internet sites or on other Web sites they may link to. Any comments or suggestions can be sent by e-mail to comments@enslow.com or to the address on the back cover.

Cover Illustration: Time Life Pictures/ Getty Images.

Photos and Illustrations: AP/ Wide World Photos, pp. 4, 56, 79, 97, 99; courtesy of the Walton family and Wal-Mart Archives, pp. 6, 14, 18, 24, 27, 32, 36; Getty Images, pp. 10, 44, 47, 86, 92; Rogers Historical Museum, p. 88; Time Life Pictures /Getty Images, pp. 1, 69, 75.

CONTENTS

Sam Walton

1
GAMBLING ON LIFE

There **was something different** about Sam Walton, founder of the giant Wal-Mart chain. At age sixty-four, he was still an active, pleasant man with a slender build and a shock of white hair hidden beneath his Wal-Mart baseball cap. But over the past few years, Walton's energy had slumped.

No one was particularly alarmed. By 1982, Walton had been working for more than forty years to become a retail powerhouse. His work schedule was grueling enough to exhaust a man half his age. On most days, he was up before dawn and worked late into the night. He crisscrossed the Midwest in his airplane to visit his stores or search for new locations. On Saturday mornings, a day of rest for many, Walton was up by 4:00 A.M. reviewing sales figures for his weekly Saturday morning meeting.

Twenty years after opening his first Wal-Mart store in 1962, Sam Walton's retail venture grew into a 551-store chain.

While many men his age were looking ahead to retirement, he was focused only on improving his stores.

Walton had taken his first tentative steps into the world of discounting by opening the first Wal-Mart in 1962. His competitive nature kept him constantly at work, fine-tuning his operation. He was always looking ahead to the next store, the next town, the next goal. He adopted an almost religious fervor about finding ways to reduce the company's expenses so he could charge less for his merchandise. In 20 years, that first unimpressive Wal-Mart had grown into a chain of 551 stores in 15 states. Walton was eager to keep going, if only his strength could hold out.

Walton tried cutting back on his hectic pace at work. He turned over some of his responsibilities to others. He took more time to travel with his wife and to enjoy his two favorite hobbies—tennis and bird hunting. Nothing helped. He still tired easily and his energy level sagged even lower.

Finally, Walton visited his doctor. The results were distressing. Blood tests showed that he had an alarming lack of white blood cells. The cause was a rare type of blood cancer called hairy cell leukemia. The disease was destroying his white blood cells—the ones his body needed to fight off infections. The doctor told Walton that his leukemia had been developing slowly for the past six or seven years.

Hairy cell leukemia gets its name from the hairlike projections seen poking out of the abnormal cells when viewed under a microscope. It is a rare form of leukemia, making up a small percentage of all blood cancer cases. People do not usually die from hairy cell leukemia itself, but their bodies can become unable to fight off life-threatening infections.

Being sick was something new for Walton. He was normally healthy, athletic, and in control. When problems arose in business, he was usually able to find a solution. But this was different. This time his body was calling the shots. All Walton could do was hope there was a way to stop the disease.

On his doctor's advice, Walton flew to M.D. Anderson Hospital, a renowned cancer research hospital in Houston, Texas. After being poked, prodded, and examined for three days, the doctors confirmed Walton's diagnosis. His case was turned over to Dr. Jorge R. Quesada, an authority on hairy cell leukemia.

Quesada recommended the standard treatment for Walton. It involved surgery to remove his spleen, an organ which filters the blood and helps the body fight infections. The surgery would be followed by chemotherapy to kill off any remaining cancer cells.

Walton refused. "He said he wouldn't have surgery," said Quesada. "He was adamant. He was not going to let us remove his spleen. He said no—absolutely!"[1]

Quesada did not try to change Walton's mind. He knew that only about 25 percent of the people having the standard treatment would still be alive five years later. There was another option open, but it was strictly experimental. Quesada was testing a new biological substance called interferon. At that time, the substance was unproven, difficult to get, and extremely expensive.

Interferon was not a drug, but a combination of fifteen proteins taken from white blood cells. Less than a quarter teaspoon of powdered interferon could treat a patient for three months. However, it took three hundred blood donors to produce that tiny amount. The cost was about ten thousand dollars a month. Walton could easily handle the expense, but dealing with the risk was another matter.

Would it work? Quesada had only tried interferon on ten patients with hairy cell leukemia, but he was encouraged by the results. Still, there were no guarantees. Every person is different and no one could say exactly what interferon's effect would be on Walton.

Although he hated the idea of surgery, Walton was not sure he wanted to be a guinea pig for a research project. He told Quesada that he would have to think about it. He flew back to Bentonville to wrestle with the difficult decision.

"Predominantly, he wanted to be sure the treatment wouldn't interfere with his extraordinarily busy schedule," Quesada recalled.[2]

Back in Bentonville, Walton stewed about his situation. He was a private man who did not share much of his personal life with others. But news of a life-threatening disease was too big to keep to himself. He needed to break the news to his Wal-Mart "family," which by then included 41,000 "associates," as all company employees were called. It was a struggle to get the words down on paper. It took him two or three tries over two days to get the words right. His letter appeared in the October 1982 issue of the company magazine, *Wal-Mart World.*

In his letter, Walton told his associates about his visit to M.D. Anderson Hospital and the tests that had been run. He then revealed the diagnosis of hairy cell leukemia. Walton apologized for discussing personal matters and expressed his confidence that the

Sam Walton leads Wal-Mart employees in the famous "Wal-Mart cheer."

treatment would be successful. He told them he would still be coming around for visits and doing the other things he enjoyed.[3]

A month went by and Walton still had not made up his mind about the treatment. He returned to Houston to ask Quesada more questions. While there, he received one piece of good news. Scientists had discovered a way to make a synthetic version of interferon. This made the substance more available and much less expensive.

Even after the second visit, Walton was still not 100 percent sure he wanted to try interferon. He went home to think about if for another month. Finally, he decided to take the risk.

The interferon treatment was fairly simple. For the first six months, Walton would receive a daily injection, given either by himself or a family member. For the next six months, the injections were only required three times a week. Before the treatment was half over, Walton's leukemia went into remission. His energy returned and he had experienced no side effects. Interferon had been a success.

Walton did not know what incredible things the future held for him. At least now he was healthy enough to tackle whatever came along.

2

THE BOY FROM KINGFISHER

Kingfisher was little more than a dot on the plains of Oklahoma, but it had been home to Thomas Walton most of his life. He did not remember his parents, who had died when he was very young. Under the guidance of relatives, Thomas grew into an industrious and intelligent young man.

Walton began working for his uncle in the farm mortgage business. While still in his twenties, he bought a farm on the outskirts of town. By that time, he had fallen in love with eighteen-year-old Nannia Lee Lawrence. The two were married in 1917. On March 29, 1918, the young couple welcomed their first son into the family. He was named Samuel Moore Walton, after the grandfather he never knew. Three years later, Sam's younger brother, James, better known as Bud, joined the family. Sam and Bud were close as children and remained close their entire lives.

Sam was a bright, curious child. One day when he was three years old, he wandered away from home. His frantic mother finally found him at the local schoolhouse, where he was attentively listening to the teacher.

At first, Thomas Walton made a good living on the farm. World War I was raging, and surplus food was needed in war-torn Europe. But soon after Sam was born, the war ended. Farmers in Europe were able to grow their own food again. Americans were left with huge surpluses, causing crop prices to tumble. Sam's father could no longer make enough money farming to care for his young family. He returned to the farm mortgage business.

When Sam was five, the Waltons moved to Springfield, Missouri, where Sam started school. His father had the unpleasant job of repossessing farms from families who could not pay back their loans. It was hard, but Thomas Walton did it in a way that left the families with as much self-respect as possible. He was known to be honest and fair in his dealings.

Sam's family did not have a lot of money, but they were better off than most Americans at that time. The country was in the grip of the Great Depression, a period when jobs were scarce and poverty was widespread. It was even worse for farmers in Oklahoma

Sam Walton as a newborn. Sam was a bright, curious child.

and other states in the plains. The combination of a devastating drought and poor farming techniques led to crop failures. Great winds blew across the dry land destroying valuable topsoil. Great dust storms turned the skies black and made breathing difficult. The area became known as the Dust Bowl. Farmers' crops failed and they were unable to pay their bills. Many lost their farms.

Thomas Walton's job kept him on the road most of the time. Sam sometimes went along when his father had to repossess a farm. He saw firsthand what it was like to live in poverty. It was an impression that remained with him always.[1]

Although the Waltons did not live in poverty, they had to be careful with their finances. Sam learned that money was something to be worked for and spent wisely. He began working at odd jobs while he was still in elementary school. He sold magazine subscriptions and raised

The Great Depression

From 1929 to 1941, the United States experienced a severe economic crisis, called the Great Depression. The stock market crashed in 1929, causing huge losses for investors.

During the worst years of the Depression, from 1932 to 1933, 25 to 30 percent of the people who wanted to work could not find jobs. A lot of families lost their homes and farms when they could not pay back their loans. Millions of people could not even afford to buy food. With no one to buy their products, factories closed and more businesses failed. This put even more people out of work and extended the circle of poverty.

World War II eventually ended the Depression in 1940. The market was stimulated by the need to build planes, tanks, weapons, and other defense items.

rabbits and pigeons for sale. In the seventh grade, he started delivering newspapers.

Things were not always calm in the Walton household. "Mother and Dad were two of the most quarrelsome people who ever lived together," Sam said. "As the oldest child, I felt like I took a lot of the brunt of this domestic discord."[2] Sam believed that his parents only stayed together because of the two boys.

The Walton family moved several times while Sam was growing up, but he made friends easily wherever he went. He loved sports and anything that sparked his competitive nature. When he joined the Boy Scouts, Sam bet his friends that he would be the first one in the group to reach the rank of Eagle Scout. He was only thirteen when he reached his goal, making him the youngest Eagle Scout Missouri had ever had up to that time.

Sam's Boy Scout training was put to good use during a class picnic. A classmate, Donald Peterson, fell into the Salt River, which was swollen from recent rains. Donald was swept into the deep water and screamed for help. Sam quickly dove into the water and swam against the swift current. Just as Donald was going down for the fifth time, Sam grabbed him from behind and pulled him to shore. Donald was unconscious and turning blue. Sam used the first-aid techniques he had learned in scouts to revive his friend.

Nan Walton had high expectations for her sons.

She encouraged them to do their best in everything they tried. She was also determined that her sons would go to college. Her own college days had been cut short when she quit after one year to get married.[3]

When Sam was getting ready to begin his sophomore year in high school in 1933, the family moved to Columbia, Missouri. It was a college town, home to the University of Missouri. The Waltons bought a large two-story brick home and rented three of the upstairs bedrooms to university students.

Sam took the move in stride, and quickly adjusted to life at Hickman High School. He joined every club he could find. In spite of his small stature, Sam's competitiveness and his belief in teamwork made him good at sports. During his senior year, he was the starting quarterback for Hickman's football team. He led them to the state title in 1935. His basketball team also won the state championship his senior year.

High school was a busy time for Sam. By then, he was making his own money and buying his own clothes. He milked the cow before school and delivered the milk to customers in the neighborhood after football practice. He also kept up with his paper route.

Sam's friendliness made him popular at school. He was elected vice president of his junior class and president of the student council his senior year. There was a full-page picture of him in the yearbook his senior year naming him "Most Versatile Boy."

Senior portrait photograph of Sam Walton from his high school yearbook.

"Sam was a hard worker. He was optimistic all the time. He had a great smile on his face and felt like everybody was his friend and the world was something he could conquer," said Clay Cooper, who played football with Sam at Hickman.[4]

In 1936, Walton graduated from high school and began studying at the University of Missouri. He was friendly and spoke to everyone he passed on the street. As a result, he was well known on campus. He joined a fraternity, Beta Theta Pi, and became active in many campus organizations. The student body elected him president his senior year.

Since his family did not have enough money to pay for college, Walton put himself through school. He not only delivered the daily *Columbia Missourian,* he was the newspaper's number one salesman all through college. His fraternity brothers nicknamed him Hustler Walton because of his salesmanship.

Walton also waited tables at the university in return for food. During the summers, he worked as a lifeguard at a public pool and organized a swim team. With all his jobs, Walton made enough money to pay his college expenses and even buy a car.

As graduation neared, Walton had to decide what to do with the rest of his life. He thought about going to graduate school, but decided that it was too expensive. Going into the insurance business was also a possibility. Finally, he decided to try retailing.

3
NOT CUT OUT
FOR RETAIL?

Three days after graduating from the University of Missouri with a degree in economics, Walton started his career in retailing. He worked as a management trainee at a J. C. Penney store in Des Moines, Iowa, for seventy-five dollars a month. Walton loved working with the customers, but did not like taking time away from them to do his paperwork. One of his supervisors was not impressed with his sloppy record keeping.

"Walton," he would say. "I'd fire you if you were not such a good salesman. Maybe you're just not cut out for retail."[1]

Walton was determined to learn as much as he could about the retail business. He started work at 6:30 in the morning and did not quit until 7:00 or 8:00

at night. He spent his lunch hours poking around other stores to learn how they did things. On Saturdays, he and the other trainees often got together with their manager to talk shop.

One day, the store's founder, James Cash Penney, came in for a visit. He taught Walton how to wrap a package using the least amount of paper and string possible. Meeting Penney in person meant a lot to Walton. He was impressed with the older man's attention to detail and the way he put customer's satisfaction ahead of profit.[2]

Walton only worked for J. C. Penney for eighteen months. By that time, the United States was involved in World War II. Walton had received military training in college as part of ROTC (Reserve Officers Training Corps). By quitting his job, he knew he would soon be drafted into the army. He expected to be sent overseas to fight, but his physical examination changed that. Doctors found a slight irregularity in Walton's heart, which made him ineligible for combat duty. He could, however, serve in a noncombat role.

While waiting to be called for active duty, Walton worked in a gunpowder factory in Pryor, Oklahoma. The area was crowded with thousands of defense workers. Walton had to go to Claremore, nineteen miles away, to find a room to rent.

One April night in 1942, Walton was at a Claremore bowling alley. He noticed an attractive girl bowling with her date on the next lane. Her name was Helen Robson, the daughter of a wealthy Oklahoma banker and rancher.

"My date had gone up to bowl," Helen Walton recalled. "I came back to my seat and there was this fellow with his right foot hung over the seat next to me. He said, 'Haven't I seen you someplace before?'"[3]

It was a corny line, but it was enough to spark a romance. The two were a good match for each other and their relationship developed quickly. They became engaged a few months later when Walton was drafted into the army.

Walton described Helen as "pretty and smart and educated, ambitious and opinionated and strong-willed."[4]

"I always told my mother and dad that I was going to marry someone who had that special energy," Helen said later. "Maybe I overshot a little."[5]

On July 16, 1942, Walton was inducted into the army as a second lieutenant. He was sent to California for training. By that time there were two things he was certain about. He knew he wanted to marry Helen and he knew he wanted to make his living in retail.[6]

Walton took a three-day leave to marry Helen on Valentine's Day in 1943. It was a large society wedding, something Claremore was not used to during those tough times.

The newlyweds moved frequently during their

army days. Walton supervised the security for aircraft plants and prisoner of war camps in California and Utah. Helen made one extended trip home so that their first son could be born in Tulsa. Samuel Robson Walton, or Rob as he was called, arrived on October 28, 1944.

Walton's last assignment for the army was in Salt Lake City, Utah. He was already looking ahead to his future career. He made regular trips to the library to find books on retailing. He spent time studying one of the department stores in Salt Lake to see what he could learn. As soon as the war was over in 1945, Walton began looking for the best place to start his new life.

"I always told my mother and dad that I was going to marry someone who had that special energy."

A college friend of Walton's suggested that the two of them become partners in a small department store in St. Louis. It sounded good to Walton, but Helen was against it. She thought having a partner was too risky. Besides, St. Louis was much too big.

"Sam, we've been married two years, and we've moved sixteen times. Now, I'll go with you any place you want so long as you don't ask me to live in a big city. Ten thousand people is enough for me," she said.[7]

Walton met with people at Butler Brothers, a

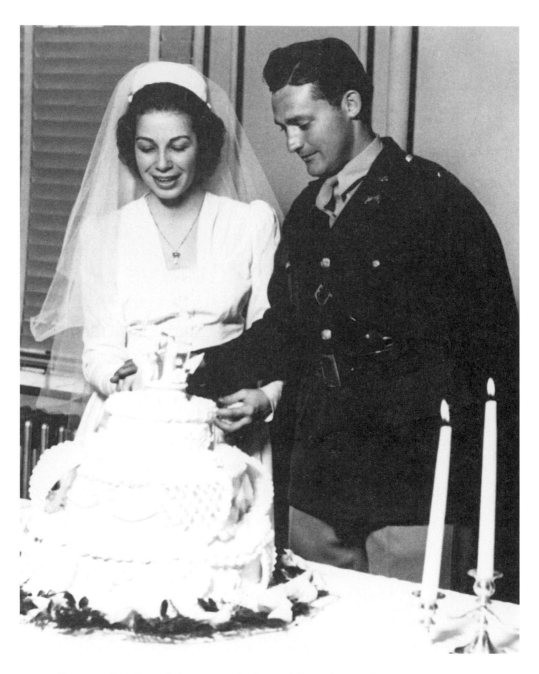

Sam and Helen Walton on their wedding day, February 14, 1943.

company that sold franchises to a chain of variety stores called Ben Franklin. They told him about a Ben Franklin store in Newport, Arkansas, that was for sale. Walton liked the looks of Newport and decided to buy the store. He used $5,000 that he had saved and borrowed $20,000 from Helen's father. He signed a five-year lease on the building the store occupied.

Newport was a pleasant town of about five thousand people built beside the White River. It was a railroad town surrounded by cotton farms and pecan orchards. Walton's store sat next to a J. C. Penney on Front Street in the center of town.

To some people, Walton's Newport store seemed like a poor choice. Not only was the store losing money, but there was a Sterling variety store right across the street. The Sterling store, owned by John Dunham, was doing twice as much business as the one Walton was buying. But Walton was not worried. He was twenty-seven years old, full of confidence, and very competitive. He set high goals for himself. He would not stop at making his store better than Dunham's store. He planned to make his store the most profitable Ben Franklin in Arkansas.[8]

"For all of my confidence I hadn't had a day's experience in running a variety store," Walton admitted.[9] In fact, he had worked in retail for only eighteen months. Owning his own store was completely different. Butler Brothers gave him two weeks of training

Dime-Store Days

Before the days of large discount stores, dime stores were the places to go for bargains. They were also called five-and-tens or five-and-dimes or went by company names like Woolworth, Kresge, or Ben Franklin. When dime stores first started back in the late nineteenth and early twentieth centuries, most items sold for only five or ten cents. As the cost of living rose in later years, so did dime-store prices.

Dime stores were full of a delightful hodgepodge of items that even a kid with a few cents could afford.

Dime stores began to disappear in the 1960s when large discount stores became popular. Today's "dollar stores" are the closest thing we have to the old-fashioned dime stores.

and loaded him up with instruction books to answer most of his questions. Ready or not, Walton opened his store on September 1, 1945.

The assistance he received from Butler Brothers was valuable, but Walton did not agree with all their rules. If he wanted to get the hefty rebates they offered, he had to buy at least 80 percent of his merchandise from them. Walton did not like paying their higher prices. He had already figured out that the best way to attract customers was to sell items for less. He could not do that if he had to pay the high markups demanded by Butler Brothers.

Walton was smart enough to figure out how much he could get away with. He found some manufacturers who would sell him items direct for less money. On many nights after his store closed, Walton hooked up a homemade trailer to his station wagon and drove to Tennessee. He filled his trailer with bargains, then drove home. The new merchandise would be on sale in his store the next day.

One of Walton's bargain items was ladies underwear. He was able to buy a dozen pair for $2.00 instead of the usual $2.50. Instead of selling three pair for a dollar, he sold four pair for the same price. Women piled into the store to snatch up the bargains. Walton had learned an important lesson. By selling for less, he could increase sales so much that he actually earned more money.

Walton learned early on that rolling back prices was the best way to win customers and, ultimately, increase long-term profits.

Walton's competitiveness kept him constantly looking for ways to improve his store. He spent his spare time snooping around other stores to see how they did things. Many of his visits were to Dunham's store across the street. If Walton found a product that Dunham was selling for less money, he hurried back to his own store and lowered his price on the same item.

"Sam was always over there checking on John. Always. Looking at his prices, looking at his displays, looking at what was going on. . . . I'm sure it aggravated him quite a bit early on," Helen Walton said.[10]

Saturdays were the biggest shopping days in Newport. Farmers flocked into town to stock up on supplies. The bustling streets gave the town a festive feeling. Walton found gimmicks to attract more shoppers to his store. He put his popcorn machine outside on the sidewalk. The scent of freshly popped corn drifted through the air and acted like a magnet to draw people in. The popcorn worked so well that Walton borrowed eighteen hundred dollars to buy Newport's first soft serve ice-cream machine. He did not like being in debt, but his gamble paid off. His ice-cream machine drew in even more customers.

One day, Walton heard that John Dunham was going to expand his store into a vacant space next door. Walton hurried to Hot Springs and convinced the building owner to lease the space to him instead. He was not sure exactly what he would do with it. He just knew he could not afford to let Dunham have it. With a little help, Walton put together a small department store in only six days. His new venture, called the Eagle Store, did not make much money, but it kept his competitor from expanding.

Life in Newport was good. The Walton family grew quickly with the births of sons John in 1946 and Jim in 1948, and daughter Alice in 1949. Walton became president of the Chamber of Commerce, head of the Rotary Club, active in the Presbyterian Church, and even served on the City Council for one term. Besides chasing after four energetic youngsters, Helen was active in church and other groups in the community. The Waltons made a lot of friends and their store was a huge success. Settling down in Newport had definitely been the right thing to do. That is why it came as such a shock when, in Walton's words, he was "kicked out of town."[11]

4
STARTING OVER

By 1950, **Sam Walton** was feeling the glow of success. His store in Newport had become the top Ben Franklin store, not only in Arkansas, but in a six-state region. But in the end, it was the success of his store that caused him to lose it.

When Walton signed his lease five years earlier, he did not know enough to include an option giving him the right to renew it. His landlord looked at Walton's successful store and decided that it would make a good business for his son. He refused to renew Walton's lease.

Nothing would change the landlord's mind and there were no other available spaces in Newport for Walton to move into. There was nothing left for him to do but find another town and start over.

"It was the low point of my life," Walton recalled. "I felt sick to my stomach. . . . I had built the best variety store in the whole region and worked hard in the community—done everything right—and now I was being kicked out of town. It didn't seem fair."[1]

Walton was not one to dwell on his mistakes. He learned from them, then moved on. He and Helen began looking at towns in Northwest Arkansas. They liked the area because it was close to Helen's family. Walton liked it because he could take advantage of quail-hunting seasons there. They discovered the tiny town of Bentonville nestled in the green rolling hills of the Ozark Mountains.

There was a store for sale on Bentonville's shady town square. It was not very impressive. The store was too small, and the inside was dark and gloomy. The only light came from three 100-watt bulbs dangling from the ceiling. Even worse, the store had only done $32,000 worth of business its last year. That was much less than the $250,000 worth of sales in Walton's Newport store.

Walton saw possibilities in the Bentonville store, but only if certain conditions were met. First, he insisted on buying the building. There would be no more five-year leases for him. He also insisted on a ninety-nine-year lease on the barbershop next door so that he could expand. But the owners of both buildings repeatedly turned him down.

Helen's father, L. S. Robson, was not ready to give up. Without telling Walton, he met with the owners of both buildings and finally convinced them to accept his terms. Walton could now have his new store.

On May 9, 1950, Walton signed the papers and took possession of the Bentonville store. Everything looked bright that day—except for the sky. A storm hit, dumping twelve inches of rain on Bentonville in twenty-four hours. Walton discovered that among his store's shortcomings was a leaky roof.

It took a lot of work to get the new store ready. A wall was torn out so the store could expand into the barbershop next door. Dull lightbulbs were replaced with bright fluorescent lights. New shelves and

Walton suffered several early setbacks in his career before steady success came.

counters were added. The words *WALTON'S 5¢-10¢* were spelled out in large red letters across the storefront. In spite of the store's name, Walton's new store was actually another Ben Franklin franchise.

During this time, Walton heard about two variety stores in Minnesota that were using a new idea called self-service. Up until that time, each department in a variety store had its own clerk. The clerk stood behind a counter and brought out the items the customers asked for. Customers paid separately at each counter. With self-service, customers chose what they wanted off open shelves and paid for everything at once on their way out.

Walton took an all-night bus trip to Minnesota to learn more about this idea. He liked what he saw. With self-service, he would not have to hire as many clerks. He felt that customers would buy more since they did not have to wait for someone to help them. Walton set up his Bentonville store using the new idea. It became only the third self-service variety store in the nation. All of Walton's future stores would use this system.

On July 29, 1950, Walton opened his Bentonville store with a remodeling sale. He promised free balloons to the kids and low prices on enough items to tempt their parents.

Walton's new store was open, but he still owned the Newport store until the end of the year. Traveling between stores took eight to ten hours of driving more than 250 miles of curvy Arkansas roads. At the end of the year, he closed his Newport store and the family moved to Bentonville.

Bentonville was much different than Newport, a busy cotton and railroading town. Bentonville, with a population of only three thousand, not only lacked a railroad, it did not even have a traffic light. But it was not long before the family became part of the community. Walton helped start a Little League baseball program and sponsored the high-school football team. He became active in several civic organizations, taught Sunday school, and was also an elder in the Presbyterian church.

Soon after settling in Bentonville, Walton began thinking about opening another store. In 1952, he learned that a small grocery store was closing in Fayetteville, Arkansas, twenty miles away. Even though there were already two variety stores on the square, Walton decided it was a good location for his second store. He hired a manager to help run it.

In 1954, Walton discovered another new idea in retail. A shopping center was going up in Ruskin Heights, near Kansas City, Missouri. It included a 100,000-square-foot cluster of stores surrounded by ample parking. Shopping centers were almost unheard of at that time. The Ruskin Heights center was only the second center to be built in the United States. Walton and his brother Bud went together to buy the Ben

Franklin franchise. The store was a tremendous success, doing $250,000 in sales and earning $30,000 in profit the first year.

Walton was so excited about the success of the shopping center that he decided to try developing a center of his own. He found a forty-acre site in Little Rock and set out to find financial backers. At that time, no investors wanted to get involved in something as risky as a shopping center. They were not sure the idea would ever catch on. After spending two years and more $25,000 trying to put deals together, Walton finally gave up. He had learned a lot about real estate, but it was an expensive lesson.

Now that Walton had stores in several towns, he spent a lot of time driving between them. That meant spending hours on the narrow, winding roads of Arkansas. It occurred to Walton that flying would save him a lot of time.

One day, Walton invited Bud to go look at an airplane with him. Bud Walton knew about flying. He had been a Navy pilot during World War II. He also knew that his brother was not the most careful driver in a car. He was afraid Sam would kill himself in an air-plane. Bud refused to go look at the plane, hoping that would discourage Sam from flying.

In spite of his brother's protests, Walton was determined to fly. He bought a dilapidated two-seater with a small engine. Bud was not impressed with his

By the late 1950s, Walton was flying in his own plane in order to travel more quickly between his stores. Flying would prove a boon to his business.

brother's purchase. "It had a washing machine motor in it, and it would putt-putt, and then miss a lick, then putt-putt again," he said.[2] "The old radio was a crank job, and it would have been just as effective to open the cockpit door and use a megaphone to communicate."[3]

It was two years before Bud Walton got into the plane. The two brothers flew to Little Rock. Bud worried the whole way that the plane would fall apart before they got there.[4]

Flying was a boon to Walton's business. It not only

made it easier to get to his stores, it allowed him to look for potential store sites along the way. One day, while flying to St. Louis, Walton noticed a lot of traffic around Waynesville, Missouri. The town was home to the Fort Leonard Wood Army Reserve. Walton believed that with all the soldiers and their families, the area would be a good place for a Ben Franklin. As soon as he landed, he called Bud and told him to check out the area.

Bud Walton could not find a place flat enough to build a store in Waynesville. He drove to nearby St. Robert. He saw bulldozers leveling out an area for a grocery store. The store owner happened to be standing by his truck nearby. Before the afternoon was over, Bud had convinced the owner to expand the size of his store and lease part of it to the Waltons.

Walton designed a larger store for St. Robert, and called it Walton's Family Center. He was breaking new ground. No other independent variety chain had tried putting a large store in a small town. The store opened in 1962 and did amazingly well.

Adding more stores made Walton busier than ever. Still, he and Helen worked hard to pass along their values to their children. All four of them began working at an early age. Alice helped sell popcorn and ice cream at her father's store when she was only five. The boys helped clean the store and carried boxes. The children were encouraged to invest their money in the stores.

Hula Hoops

In the late 1950s, hula hoops were the latest craze among kids across the country. It was hard for smaller stores to get hula hoops, and they were expensive. But that was not going to stop Walton. He and Jim Dodson, the owner of another variety store, decided to make their own.

On certain nights, the two men set up an assembly line in the attic after their stores closed. They loaded up on colorful plastic pipe purchased from a small company. The men cut the pipe into pieces nine feet long. They used a plug to join the ends together, then stapled them in place.

Working together, Walton and Dodson could make several thousand hula hoops in a single night. The hoops sold for about a dollar and each new batch sold out quickly.

The family also made time for fun. They often took camping trips in the Ozark Mountains. For several years, they took month-long vacations. Their old DeSoto station wagon was crammed with four kids and a dog with a canoe strapped to the top. Camping equipment was carried in a homemade trailer attached to the back. No matter where the family went, Walton insisted on visiting stores along the way.

One summer, the family went to the East Coast. They attracted a lot of attention driving into New York City. People there were not used to seeing a car topped by a canoe and pulling a trailer in the middle of the busy city. The family also attracted attention when they attended a Broadway musical that night. While the New Yorkers in the audience were dressed in their furs and formals, the Waltons wore Bermuda shorts.

Besides passing on his values, Walton wanted to give his children financial security. He took the advice of his father-in-law and set up a family partnership. All the profits from his stores went into the partnership. Each child owned 20 percent while Sam and Helen Walton owned the other 20 percent. At first there was not much money in the partnership, but in later years the amount grew into billions of dollars.

Walton was successful, in part, because he kept an eye on what was happening in the retail business. By 1960, he was aware of a trend that could spell disaster for his variety stores: discount stores. Instead of selling just a few items at a discount, they sold everything at a reduced price. Walton knew that his variety stores would have a hard time competing with them.

Discounting was not a new concept. There had been discount stores in New England since the 1940s. But those were individual stores. By the end of the 1950s, discount chains began to spring up.

The biggest threat to Walton's variety stores came from Gibson's, a discount chain found mostly in Arkansas and Texas. When Gibson's put a store in Fayetteville, Walton knew it was time to act. "[I] really had only two choices left: stay in the variety store business, which I knew was going to be hit hard by the discounting wave of the future; or open a discount store."[5]

5
BIRTH OF
A GIANT

The year 1962 could be called the year of the discounters. It marked the birth of four large discount chains. K-Mart opened its first store as part of S. S. Kresge, which operated a chain of eight hundred variety stores. Woolco began as part of the nation's largest variety store chain, F. W. Woolworth. Target began as part of the Dayton-Hudson Corporation, a regional department store chain. And Wal-Mart opened as part of—nothing!

Sam Walton was one lone man going up against giants. He did not have a huge corporation behind him to provide leadership and start-up money. He did not have suppliers lined up to fill his stores with merchandise. All Walton had was a fierce determination to succeed and a few secrets he had picked up while operating his sixteen variety stores.

Walton was already a discounter at heart. He knew that there was money to be made by selling a high volume of items at lower prices. He had spent two years visiting discount stores around the country to see how they did things. Walton cornered the people in charge and bombarded them with questions. To them, Walton was just a pleasant man from a backwater town in Arkansas. They did not see any harm in sharing information with him.

Other discounters did not consider Walton a threat. But Walton knew something they did not. He knew that small towns were an untapped market. The others believed that their stores would only succeed in areas with large populations, such as cities and their suburbs. But Walton had seen how successful his family centers had become in small towns. "If we offered prices as good or better than stores in cities that were four hours away by car, people would shop at home," he said.[1]

Walton believed in discounting, but he did not want to jump into it by himself. Since he already had a working relationship with Butler Brothers, he traveled to Chicago to see if they would back him in his new venture. He hoped they would agree to supply his new stores, just as they were doing with his variety stores. But when the executives found out that they would have to settle for half their profit margin, they turned him down flat. "They blew up!" Walton said later. "They just couldn't see the philosophy."[2]

Next Walton headed to Dallas to discuss the matter with Herbert Gibson Sr. Perhaps he could buy a Gibson's franchise or work a deal to buy merchandise through their volume-buying program. Walton showed up at Gibson's office unannounced. Gibson kept him waiting for five hours before finally agreeing to talk to him. Walton was again turned down. Gibson saw him as a small-time variety store owner with neither the money nor the experience to run one of his stores.

Walton tried others, but always with the same disappointing results. No one else shared his belief that putting discount stores in small towns would work. If he wanted to go into discounting, he would have to do it on his own.

Finding enough money to build the first store was a problem. No one wanted to invest money in Walton's crazy idea. Bud Walton agreed to invest only 3 percent of the necessary amount, and Don Whitaker, the manager, put in 2 percent. Walton and Helen had to come up with 95 percent of the cost. In a very risky move, they borrowed enough money to build a 16,000-square-foot store. If the business failed and they could not pay back their loan, they could lose their home.

On July 2, 1962, the first Wal-Mart opened in nearby Rogers, Arkansas. The dumpy-looking store was small. Merchandise was stacked haphazardly on tables and hung on a few racks. Much of the merchandise was of poor quality because Walton had a hard time finding companies that would sell to him at a discount. "We were the victims of a good bit of arrogance from a lot of vendors in those days. They did not need us, and they acted that way," Walton admitted.[3]

In spite of everything, shoppers filled the store to scoop up the advertised bargains. On opening day, they could buy a Sunbeam iron for $11.88 instead of the usual $17.95. A Wilson baseball glove was only $5.97 instead of the $10.80 list price. A $100 Polaroid camera sold for $74.37.

Not everyone was excited about the opening of Wal-Mart. Executives at Butler Brothers were upset that Walton's new business was competing with the Ben Franklin store in Rogers. Officials from Chicago marched into the store on opening day and met with Walton in his office. They told him in no uncertain terms not to open any more Wal-Marts. Walton was not intimidated by their demands.

Since Walton was starting his discount business by himself, he had to work harder than his competition. He had to learn more about setting up and running larger stores. He had to search harder to find merchandise to sell. Most important, he had to find the cheapest way to do everything in order to keep his

Sam Walton sitting at his desk in his personal office.

costs down. His efforts paid off by making him a better retailer.

Walton waited for two years to see how the first Wal-Mart did before he opened another one. Sales during the first year reached $700,000. That was three times as much as his average variety stores, but not as much as the $2 million in sales at the Walton's Family Center in St. Roberts. Still, the first store was successful enough to convince Walton to open another one.

The second Wal-Mart opened in Harrison, Arkansas, in 1964. It was located on a former cattle auction yard. The drafty 12,000-square-foot building had a concrete floor and an eight-foot ceiling. Merchandise was displayed on wooden planks bought from a bankrupt variety store. There were no restrooms.

The opening for the Harrison store was as unpleasant as the store itself. Walton had set up a display of watermelons outside the store. He also brought in

Near Miss

In May 1969, Walton took Ron Mayer on a plane ride to show him Wal-Mart's operation in Carthage, Missouri. Just as Walton touched down at the Carthage airport, a small plane pulled onto the runway directly ahead of him. Walton's plane was barreling down the runway at fifty miles an hour. Walton immediately revved his engines and pulled back on the yoke. At the last moment, his plane lifed off the runway and passed over the other plane.

"Our wheels didn't clear that student plane more than a foot. It was unbelievable!" Mayer recalled. "It was the closest I ever came to getting killed in an airplane."[4]

In spite of almost being killed, Mayer eventually went to work for Wal-Mart.

donkeys for the children to ride in the parking lot. David Glass, a businessman that Walton was trying to hire, was not impressed. "It was 115 degrees, and the watermelons began to pop, and the donkeys began to do what donkeys do, and it all mixed together and ran all over the parking lot," Glass said. "It was the worst retail store I had ever seen."[5]

Needless to say, Glass turned down the job offer. "He was a nice fellow, but I wrote him off. It was just terrible," Glass said.[6] Little did he know that years later, he would be running Wal-Mart.

During the early years, Walton had only a few regular suppliers. His specials consisted of whatever he could get a good deal on that particular week. For the opening of the third Wal-Mart in Springdale, Arkansas, he had gotten a good price on Crest toothpaste and Prestone antifreeze. He sold the toothpaste for 27 cents a tube and the antifreeze for $1.00 a gallon. So many shoppers showed up that the fire department had to lock the doors and only let more customers in when others had left. To speed things up, Walton began checking people out himself, using a tackle box for a cash register.

In spite of Wal-Mart's unglamorous beginning, the chain survived and grew. The key to its success was Walton's determination to keep prices low. "When customers thought of Wal-Mart, they should think of low prices, and satisfaction guaranteed. They could be pretty sure they wouldn't find it cheaper anywhere else, and if they didn't like it, they could bring it back," he said.[7]

It was Walton's penny-pinching ways that allowed him to keep his prices lower than that of his competitors. He refused to pay high rents, so he had to settle for locations that no one else wanted. He did not use an expensive public relations firm to handle his advertising. Instead, Walton and his managers cut pictures of various products out of newspapers. They

When I Die Bury Me At WAL-MART So My HUSBAND Will Come Visit Me...

A humorous bumper sticker on display at the Wal-Mart museum. It is good example of one the store's early marketing efforts.

pasted the pictures onto a piece of paper and added their own prices.

Walton did not waste money hiring an expensive marketing firm to find the best locations for new stores. He counted cars on the town square or main street and in his competitors' parking lots. He flew over areas to scout for promising spots. "We could check out traffic flows, see which way cities and towns were growing, and evaluate the location of the competition—if there was any," he explained.[8]

During his scouting missions, Walton flew his plane low or even sideways, to get a better look at the land beneath him. "I guarantee you not many principals of retailing companies were flying around sideways studying development patterns, but it worked really well for us," he said.[9]

Walton's decision to stick to small towns with populations of five thousand to twenty-five thousand was paying off. By the end of 1969, he had opened eighteen Wal-Marts. He also still owned fourteen variety stores. His stores filled a need for rural communities while allowing Walton to avoid direct competition with the larger chains.

In spite of Wal-Mart's success, there were problems. Walton lacked an efficient system for getting merchandise into the stores. The store managers ordered what they needed, then waited until a truck could deliver it to them. It cost more to get trucks to come to their small towns, which were not on their regular routes. Also, the trucks usually delivered merchandise in amounts that were too large for the small stores to handle.

"In the boondocks, we didn't have the distributors falling over themselves to serve us," Walton said. "Our only alternative was to build a warehouse so we could buy in volume."[10]

Walton rented a warehouse in Bentonville where large deliveries could be made. Workers broke down the large orders into smaller shipments, then hired trucks to deliver the merchandise to the stores. The warehouse helped the situation, but the system needed improvement.

Walton hired Bob Thornton, who had been managing the distribution center for a dime-store chain. Thornton helped design a 100,000-square-foot warehouse. Since the employees in Bentonville were complaining about their offices in an old garage, Walton agreed to include new offices in the warehouse.

Thornton fully agreed with the need for new offices. His own office had been made by knocking down a wall into space above the shoe store next door. His cramped workspace had no heating or air-conditioning.

Walton's frugal nature made Thornton's job more difficult. Without telling Thornton, Walton had the architects reduce the size of the warehouse to 60,000 square feet.

Size was not the only issue. Thornton had designed the warehouse with tracks on the floor that would make loading and unloading the trucks easier. This "towline" system would add $60,000 to the cost. Walton saw that as an unnecessary expense.

Thornton stood his ground. "If we don't get one, then I don't belong here, because I don't know how to run a distribution center without one," he told Walton.[11] The towline stayed.

The much-needed distribution center and headquarters opened in November 1969. When asked about locating the headquarters in Bentonville, Walton told *Forbes* magazine, "The best thing we ever did was to hide back there in the hills and eventually build a company that makes folks want to find us. . . . We're much better off than if we'd gone to Chicago."[12]

Wal-Mart flourished as more stores opened. Walton was on a roll and nothing could stop him now, except one thing—money.

6

GOING PUBLIC

Sam Walton was in a panic.[1] He had taken out so many personal loans to pay for new Wal-Marts that, at one point, his family was over $2 million in debt. If, for any reason, he could not pay back his loans, the Waltons could lose nearly everything, including their home.

One day in August 1969, Walton's shaky financial situation nearly turned disastrous. Payment on one of his loans was due that day. Walton flew to his bank in Dallas to get the money he needed, but the bank refused to give him any. In desperation, he called James Jones, his former banker and financial consultant. Jones had recently become president of a bank in New Orleans. He told Walton to get back in his plane and fly to New Orleans. Jones loaned Walton enough money to cover his payment.

This crisis was over, but how long could Walton keep this up? Banks were not willing to loan money to someone so deeply in debt. Without their loans, Walton could not continue to add new stores.

There was one way the Waltons could wipe out their debt, but it had drawbacks. They could allow the public to buy shares of the company on the stock market. Wal-Mart would then be owned by the stockholders who would share in the profits and vote on some important company decisions. Walton did not like the idea of giving up control of his company.

There was another problem. The Waltons were private people who liked to keep their personal business to themselves. Going public would change that. "I just hated the idea that we were going to put all our financial interests out there for everybody to see," Helen Walton said later. "When you go public, they can ask all kinds of questions, and the family gets involved. We just became an open book, and I hated it."[2]

Going public was a last resort, but it was the only way to get out of debt and to keep Wal-Mart growing. On October 1, 1970, three hundred thousand shares of Wal-Mart stock were offered to the public. The sale brought in $4.6 million. That was more than enough to pay off Walton's debts with plenty left over for Wal-Mart's expansion. By keeping a large percentage of the stock for themselves, the Walton family kept control of the company.

With Walton's financial problems solved, Wal-Mart's expansion picked up speed. In 1971, fourteen new stores were added, bringing the total to fifty-one. Instead of opening stores all over the country, Walton systematically placed his stores within a day's drive of a warehouse. This allowed the stores to be restocked more efficiently.

As the number of stores increased, Walton had to work harder to maintain personal contact with all of them. He could not have done it without his airplanes. He spent several days a week flying to stores, often taking others along with him. Some of Walton's habits made his passengers nervous. Once airborne, he liked to put the plane on autopilot. It startled some guests to see Walton get up during a flight and walk to the restroom in the back of the plane. Others disliked his habit of working on his paperwork during a flight, especially if they had to help.

"I took the copilot's seat to enjoy the vista," wrote Tim Crane, a Wal-Mart manager. "I should have known better. If you're around Mr. Sam, you are gonna work. I found myself taking notes and sorting papers as Mr. Sam took advantage of the autopilot to review district manager reports."[3]

Visits from "Mr. Sam" were big events for store employees. He would arrive, wearing his Wal-Mart baseball cap and his plastic Wal-Mart name badge identifying him simply as "Sam." After grabbing some snacks, he would sit down with hourly employees to find out what was really going on in their store. Walton listened closely to their comments and suggestions. He heaped praise on those who were doing a good job and rarely criticized anyone. By treating his workers with respect, Walton earned their loyalty. "It is the most motivated large work force of its kind, which has a lot to do with curtailing costs," said retail consultant Peter Monash.[4]

One night, Walton showed up at a loading dock at 2:30 A.M. with a box of doughnuts. During his visit with the workers, he learned that they needed more showers at the center. He quickly took care of their request.

Walton received high marks for the way he treated his employees—except for one area. He was generous in paying his top people, but his hourly employees earned low wages. This practice made some workers think about joining a union.

A labor union acts as a middleman between employees and their employers. It tries to get higher wages, better working conditions, and better benefits for its members. If the union cannot get what it wants from an employer, its members can vote to go on strike.

Walton was adamant about keeping labor unions out of Wal-Mart. He had always encouraged Wal-Mart employees to discuss problems with their store managers or executives all the way up to Walton himself. His phone number was listed in the local Bentonville phone book for anyone to find. He did not want unions interfering with that relationship.

"They have put management on one side of the fence, employees on the other, and themselves in the middle as almost a separate business, one that depends on division between the other two camps. And divisiveness, by breaking down direct communication, makes it harder to take care of customers," he said.[5]

Walton's problems with unions began after opening a store in Mexico, Missouri, in 1970. The Retail Clerks Union tried to get the store employees to join. Walton convinced them that they were better off without the union. The employees voted against joining.

A few months later, Walton and others were setting up a new store in Clinton, Missouri. Union officials demanded that they be allowed to set up the fixtures. Walton put them off for a while. That night, he and his crew covered the windows with brown paper. They worked all night and got everything set up for the store opening. Angry union members set up picket lines on opening day. Someone put a sign in the window that read: STRIKE SALE. Shoppers crowded past the picketers and into the store. Walton had won another round, but Wal-Mart's union troubles were far from over.

Helen Walton once told her husband that he should be doing more for the clerks and other hourly

Helen Walton at a Wal-Mart shareholders' meeting in 1992. Helen influenced Sam that he needed to do more for his employees.

employees. When he began having run-ins with unions, he realized that she was right. He needed to keep his employees happy so they would not feel the need for a union.

In 1971, Wal-Mart began a profit sharing plan for the employees. The company contributed money to the employee's account, which they received when they left Wal-Mart. Employees were also allowed to buy Wal-Mart stock at a reduced price. They received bonuses for special accomplishments, such as high sales or a reduction in theft. Wal-Mart was one of the first companies to offer these benefits to its hourly workers.

Walton wanted his employees to feel that they were an important part of Wal-Mart's success. He began referring to them as "associates," a term of respect borrowed from J. C. Penney. Walton treated his associates as partners by sharing information about their store. In other companies, that information would only be seen by management.

Walton encouraged his associates to share their ideas for improving their stores. If an idea was especially good, he passed it on to other stores. The practice of putting greeters at the front door was suggested by an associate.

By 1974, Walton was fifty-six. For years, he had been listening to Helen's pleas for him to slow down. About that time, Ron Mayer, one of his top executives, made it clear that he wanted to run a company. If it was not going to be Wal-Mart, Mayer wanted to leave and find another company to run. Walton did not want to lose Mayer. After thinking about it for a few days, he decided to retire. Mayer took over as CEO (chief executive officer) while Walton stayed on as chairman of the board's executive committee.

Walton tried to stay out of the way and let Mayer run things. That became an impossible task. The atmosphere around Wal-Mart headquarters changed. Employees became divided between those who backed one executive over another. This split interfered with the exchange of information within the company. The family atmosphere Walton had worked so hard to build up was crumbling. Finally, in 1976, Walton took back his position as CEO. Mayer was not fired, but he and many of his backers chose to leave. When it was all over, about a third of the senior managers were gone.

Even during Walton's short retirement, Wal-Mart was never far from his mind. While visiting a tennis ball factory in South Korea in 1975, he watched the employees perform a company cheer. It pumped up their spirits so much that Walton decided to write one for Wal-Mart. From then on, most Wal-Mart functions began with an enthusiastic cheer, often with Walton in the lead.

"Gimme a *W*!" Walton would shout. "*W*!" the associates would yell back.

"Gimme an *A*!" he would cry. "*A*!" the associates would scream.

Then Walton proceeded through the rest of the letters in the Wal-Mart name. At the hyphen, he would shout "Gimme a squiggly!" as he squatted down and twisted his hips. The workers squiggled right back. The cheer ended with Walton shouting, "Who's number one?" and the workers shouting back "The customer!"

To many outsiders, seeing a man of Walton's stature leading a pep rally seemed strange. But Walton knew what he was doing. The Wal-Mart cheer helped build team spirit among his employees.

Saturday morning meetings were another Walton tradition. Since associates had to work on Saturdays, Walton thought the executives should too. As the company grew, several hundred executives, managers, and associates got up early to attend the 7:30 A.M. meeting.

The Saturday morning meetings always had lighthearted activities mixed in with company business. Once there was a persimmon-seed-spitting contest using a senior company manager

> **The Wal-Mart cheer helped build team spirit.**

as a target. A meeting might include a performance by the Singing Truck Drivers gospel group, or songs by Jimmy Walker and the Accountants. A celebrity guest might even show up.

Fire!

One night in April 1972, the Waltons went to bed as a thunderstorm raged outside. Suddenly, a bolt of lightning struck the house. Fire broke out in the bedroom closet.

"It was like the Fourth of July down at the Walton house!" remembered one neighbor. "Sam ran out and grabbed a hose. It was about twenty feet long, but it wasn't connected. [The fire] ruined about half the house before the firemen got it out."[7]

The Waltons rebuilt their home using the same architect that had designed the original house. The new home was similar to the old one, except that it was larger and more suitable for entertaining. While their home was being rebuilt, the Waltons lived in a double-wide mobile home on their property. Helen Walton wanted to be close so she could supervise the construction.

"He uses it for basically three purposes: to share information, to lighten everybody's load, and to rally the troops. Believe it or not, the majority of our folks wouldn't miss a Saturday morning meeting for anything," said executive vice president Al Miles.[6]

Wal-Mart's annual stockholders' meetings were also festive events. In most companies, these are boring meetings used to update stockholders and to vote on business decisions. Attendance is usually low. To boost attendance, Wal-Mart added plenty of fun to go along with the usual business. When attendance grew to more than ten thousand the meetings were moved to the arena at the University of Arkansas. The boisterous stockholders meetings were a mixture of company business, entertainment, and celebrity appearances. Wal-Mart still hosts the largest corporate annual meeting in the world.

Walton was aggressive about Wal-Mart's growth, but cautious about spending money on technology. He had to be nudged by people like David Glass, an executive vice president. Glass knew that for Wal-Mart to keep growing, it needed to improve its technology. Walton finally agreed to spend $500 million to build an up-to-date communications system.

Wal-Mart's sophisticated computer network was finished in 1977. It was so large that it took a special 16,000-square-foot building in Bentonville to house it. The system provided a rapid flow of information between the stores, the distribution centers, and the Bentonville headquarters. It allowed stores to be restocked quickly. It also made it easier for the executives to know exactly what was happening in each store.

In 1971, Walton had predicted that Wal-Mart would do over a billion dollars worth of business by 1980. No one believed him.[8] Not only was Walton right, his goal was reached a year early. Wal-Mart sales for 1979 broke the $1 billion mark. It was the youngest firm in the United States and the only regional retailer to reach that level. "Of all the milestones we ever reached, that one probably impressed me the most," Walton said.[9]

Wal-Mart's success brought several honors to Walton. In 1979, he was named Man of the Year for the retail industry by the magazine *Retail Week*. A year later, *Financial World* chose him as the most outstanding CEO in the country. "It's the best-managed company I've ever followed, and I've looked at hundreds," says Margaret Gilliam, a vice president at the First Boston investment firm.[10]

Walton may have been a good manager, but he often had so many business matters on his mind that he forgot routine things. His secretary regularly had to track down his lost briefcase. She had to apologize to people who arrived for a meeting, only to find that Walton had flown out of town on the spur of the moment.

One of Walton's forgetful moments had the Bentonville police worried that he had been kidnapped. One Sunday, they found his car parked near the high school. His guns and clothing were on the front seat. The police raced over to Walton's house and were surprised when he answered the door. It seems he had gone hunting before church and changed clothes in his car. After church, he rode home with Helen, completely forgetting that he had driven his own car.

In spite of his quirks, Walton kept a firm hand on Wal-Mart. The company was growing quickly, and Walton wanted to keep up the momentum. Now he was faced with a risky decision that could result in a huge financial loss.

7
TACKLING THE COMPETITION

Walton could be decisive, but this decision was tougher than most. Wal-Mart was growing at a steady rate. By 1980, the chain had grown to 276 stores in 11 states. Most of the growth came from opening new stores, although Walton had acquired a small chain of 21 stores. But could he handle getting 112 stores all at one time? That was the number of Kuhn's Big K stores that were now on the market.

Buying the chain would not only boost the number of Wal-Marts, it would allow Walton to get his stores into the South. It also would keep his competitors, such as K-Mart, from snapping up the stores for themselves. But it was risky. The chain was heavily in debt and a lot of the stores were unprofitable. Walton was not sure that the good stores would do well enough to make up for the poor ones. He and his executive committee wrestled with the decision for nearly two years. When they finally voted, it ended in a tie. Walton had to make the decision himself. He decided to go for it.

Taking on the Big K stores in 1981, combined with opening 69 new Wal-Marts, put a strain on the distribution center in Searcy, Arkansas. Associates at the center had to work longer hours. Their lack of sleep made them more accident prone. For some workers, joining the Teamsters Union looked like a good way to force Wal-Mart to provide better working conditions.

Walton had not changed his negative view of unions. In the weeks before the vote, he made sure his workers knew the pitfalls of joining the Teamsters. A 90-foot-long bulletin board at the plant displayed 40 years worth of newspaper articles about the strikes, violence, and accusations of criminal activity associated with the union. Walton also held a meeting with all the workers. According to eight men who were interviewed several years later, Walton told the workers that if they voted to join the union, the warehouse would be shut down.[1] No one wanted to lose their job. On February 5, 1982, the workers voted 215 to 67 against joining the union.

Melva Harmon, a labor lawyer in Little Rock, looked back on the decision. "Searcy is sort of conservative, and there is not a lot of pro-union sentiment there. It's just that there aren't that many good jobs up there. [Wal-Mart] was a good industry and I think the people were thankful for it to be there, and they don't want to rock the boat."[2]

Walton had won another union showdown, but he realized that to keep his associates content, he needed to make some changes. The Searcy plant was enlarged and improved to handle the extra merchandise flowing through it.

The Searcy plant was just one part of Wal-Mart's distribution system that became the best in the industry. What began as a single warehouse in downtown Bentonville, evolved into a network of highly automated centers. Some covered as much as twenty-seven acres under one roof.

The work going on inside a distribution center was constant. Trucks rolled up to the unloading docks in a steady stream. Workers unloaded cartons of merchandise onto the miles of conveyor belts crisscrossing the center. Scanners read the bar code on each carton and knew exactly which store it needed to go to and which truck would get it there. As if by magic, cartons moved along the maze of conveyor belts to the correct trucks. It also helped that Wal-Mart had its own fleet of trucks so that it did not have to rely on outside trucking firms.

"Our distribution facilities are one of the keys to

our success," said David Glass. "If we do anything better than other folks, that's it."[3]

With Wal-Mart's success firmly established, Walton was ready to try something new. He experimented with a chain of drug stores and some arts-and-crafts stores, but neither idea took off. Then Walton became interested in a new type of store started by Sol Price in California. In 1976, Price had started a chain of membership wholesale clubs called Price Club. Walton saw wholesale clubs as a threat to discount stores, but also as a new opportunity to explore.

Warehouse clubs allowed small businesses and individuals to buy things at deeply discounted prices. There were no frills in these warehouses. The floors were cement, and the merchandise was stacked on wooden pallets or on steel shelves that reached nearly to the ceiling. The aisles were wide to allow forklifts to bring in merchandise, which was often kept in cartons. Goods were packaged in large quantities. In order to keep out the casual shoppers looking for just a few discounted items, consumers were required to pay a membership fee to join the club.

Walton learned all he could about these stores. He opened the first Sam's Warehouse Club near Oklahoma City in 1983. The name was later shortened to Sam's Club. Some retailers were surprised that Walton would open stores that could take business away from

Wal-Mart. However, there were many differences between the two. The prices at Sam's Club were lower than Wal-Mart, but there were fewer items to choose from. While a Wal-Mart at that time may have been selling fifty thousand or sixty thousand items, Sam's Club concentrated on selling only twenty-five hundred or three thousand items. Also, Wal-Marts were found mostly in small towns, while Sam's Clubs were more common in cities.

Walton tackled the creation of his new chain of stores with the same feeling of excitement he had experienced when he started Wal-Mart. "It was almost what you'd call a second childhood for me," he said later.[4]

Three Sam's Clubs were open by the end of 1983. Within three years, forty more had been added. Walton had already passed up his friend, Sol Price, in the number of stores. That did not mean, however, that Walton was ready to quit learning things from Price. "I guess I've stolen—I actually prefer the word 'borrowed'—as many ideas from Sol Price as from anyone else in the business," Walton admitted.[5]

On one trip, Walton's snooping got him in trouble. As he wandered through a Price Club in California, he recorded his thoughts on a small tape recorder. An employee caught him and told Walton that tape recorders were not allowed in the store. He would have to give up his tape. Walton understood, since he had the same rule in his own stores. Before handing over the tape, he attached a note to Robert Price, Sol's son. He explained that he had other information on the tape that he would like to have back. Four days later, his tape was returned with everything still on it.

That was not the only time one of Walton's store visits caused a problem. While visiting some business-men in Brazil, he went off on his own to look at a store. The store employees became suspicious of the white-haired American crawling around on the floor to measure the aisles. The police were called and Walton's host had to come and smooth things over with the officials.[6]

Even with more Sam's Clubs coming on line, Walton still devoted most of his time to Wal-Mart. He liked to find new ways to motivate his associates. One of his ideas caused him one of his most embarrassing moments.

In 1983, Walton made a bet that Wal-Mart stores could not make a profit of 8 percent for that year. If he lost the bet, he agreed to dance the hula on Wall Street in the heart of New York City's financial district. It seemed like a safe bet. Three percent profit was average for the discount retail business, and 7 percent was the best Wal-Mart had ever done. But when the figures were in, the profit was a little over 8 percent. Like it or not, Walton had a hula in his future.

Sam Walton does a hula dance outside of Merrill Lynch
headquarters in New York City on March 15, 1984.

Being Appreciated

On October 8, 1983, the town of Bentonville held the Sam and Helen Walton Appreciation Day to thank them for all they had done for the town. A reviewing stand was set up across from the old WALTON'S 5¢-10¢. There were parades and speeches and messages from President Ronald Reagan, Vice President George Bush, and Arkansas governor, Bill Clinton. Walton graciously thanked the town for all their support. "You know, our family excelled in two areas. We owed the most money at the banks, and we had the most broken bones. . . . But we always managed to get the youngsters patched up and our loans paid. We could not have done it without your patronage and support."[7]

Walton enjoyed hamming it up in front of his associates, but acting silly on Wall Street was another matter. He hoped he could sneak in and do a quick hula with David Glass videotaping the event to prove that he had done it. But Glass was not about to let his boss get off that easily. He hired three authentic hula dancers and two ukulele players and notified the press. Glass helped Walton put on a grass skirt and Hawaiian shirt over his pinstripe suit. A flower lei was looped around his neck and a crown of flowers adorned his balding head. Then Walton and the Hawaiian girls danced the hula to the music of the ukulele players. Walton's embarrassing picture appeared in newspapers all over the country.

In spite of his embarrassment over the hula incident, Walton was in favor of any silliness that would motivate his employees or bring in more customers. Store managers were encouraged to think up crazy contests or events. One brave manager wrestled a bear. Another male manager rode through the town square of Bentonville on a white horse while wearing pink tights and a blonde wig.

Motivating employees and maintaining personal contact with store workers became more difficult. By the mid-1980s, there were too many stores to visit personally. There was also too much information that needed to be circulated between the stores, distribution centers, manufacturers, and headquarters. There was so much data going back and forth that the phone lines were constantly clogged.

"With a company, the risk you run is that you grow so rapidly that it gets out of control, that you can't get your arms around it," said David Glass. "People started asking, 'How you gonna communicate with all these people when you get larger?' . . . We worried about that."[8]

Once again, the solution was in technology. After convincing Walton of the benefits, Wal-Mart built the largest privately owned satellite network in the nation. It linked all phases of the company together. Enormous amounts of data could be stored or transmitted anywhere in the network. The system kept track of all the merchandise, of what was selling and where. The system even had a closed circuit television station, allowing Walton to beam his pep talks and messages to every store at the same time. When it came to technology, Wal-Mart stayed miles ahead of its competition.

Wal-Mart may have been ahead in technology, but it was behind in placing women in upper-level jobs. Even as late as 1985, there were no women among the top forty-two executive positions and no women on the board of directors.

With encouragement from his wife and daughter, Walton appointed Hillary Rodham Clinton, wife of Arkansas's governor, Bill Clinton, to the board in 1986. Clinton's influence only helped the situation a little. By 1989, out of the company's eighty-eight top officers, only two were women. Clinton left the board in 1992 to concentrate on her husband's presidential campaign.

Walton's reluctance to place women in high positions may have blemished his image, but it had little effect on his business success. He had become one of the top retailers in the country. Through his smart business decisions and hard work, he had accumulated great wealth for himself and his family. Although he was proud of his accomplishments, he would have been happy to skip the title that he was about to earn.

8
GROWING PAINS

It was a title that most people would love to have, but it annoyed Sam Walton. In 1985, *Forbes* named him the Richest Man in America with a net worth estimated at $2.8 billion. Walton was embarrassed by the title and resented the invasion of his family's privacy. "All that hullabaloo about somebody's net worth is just stupid, and it's made my life a lot more complex and difficult," he told a reporter from *Fortune.*[1]

Walton did not act like the richest man in America, and that is why people loved to read about him. Here was a billionaire who did not give a hoot about how much money he had. He was an ordinary man who hauled his hunting dogs around in an old pickup truck. Many of Walton's clothes came from Wal-Mart.

He got a five-dollar haircut at the local barbershop and was known for not leaving a tip. Reporters and photographers flocked to Bentonville to find out more about the quirky billionaire. Walton did his best to avoid them.

"The media usually portrayed me as a really cheap, eccentric recluse, sort of a hillbilly who more or less slept with his dogs in spite of having billions of dollars stashed away in a cave," Walton complained.[2]

Most of Walton's wealth was not in the form of money that he could spend easily. It was tied up in the Wal-Mart stock he and his family owned. As the company grew and became more successful, their stock increased in value. But wealth that is based on stocks changes constantly. In October of 1987, overall stock prices suddenly plunged. Walton lost over a billion dollars. When asked how he felt about the loss, Walton replied, "It's paper anyway. It was paper when we started, and it's paper afterward."[3]

Walton stayed at the top of *Forbes*'s list of richest Americans until 1989. Then the magazine acknowledged that his wealth did not belong entirely to him. The family fortune had already been divided up among Sam and Helen Walton and their four children.

With both Wal-Mart and Sam's Club doing well, Walton once again began looking for a new challenge. His passion for visiting stores took him into a hypermart

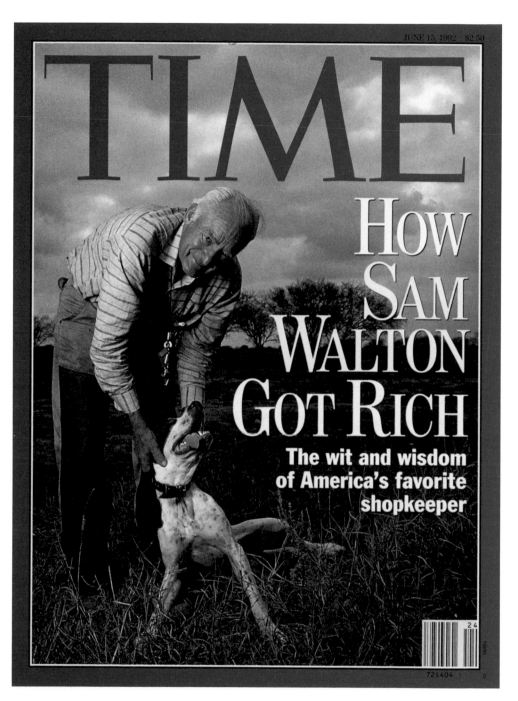

JUNE 15, 1992 $2.50

TIME

HOW SAM WALTON GOT RICH

The wit and wisdom of America's favorite shopkeeper

Sam Walton's amazing success growing his Wal-Mart chain of stores got him on the cover of several magazines, including *TIME*.

in Brazil. The gigantic store was over three times larger than the average Wal-Mart.

Hypermarts, which were becoming popular in Europe and South America, were referred to as "malls without walls." They sold food, clothing, appliances, and other merchandise. Fast-food restaurants, banks, dry cleaners, and other businesses were also located inside. The floors in hypermarts were color coded to help guide customers to the right department. Children played on indoor playgrounds while tired shoppers rested on benches. Workers often zipped around the stores on roller skates. Hypermarts were the ultimate in one-stop shopping. Customers could get a haircut, buy a refrigerator, and stock up on paper towels, all in one trip.

Walton saw hypermarts as a way to move into larger cities. They would also allow him to break into the grocery business, something he had been interested in for several years. He had avoided groceries before because he lacked experience in handling perishable foods. He solved that problem by hiring top people from some of the grocery chains.

Hypermart USA opened outside of Dallas in December 1987. The mammoth store covered 220,000 square feet of space—nearly as large as 5 football fields. But the hypermarkets were a disappointment. The enormous stores were supposed to appeal to busy people who wanted to buy everything in one place. But to weary customers, they were just too big. "In a hypermarket, by the time you've bought some aspirin, some Kleenex, and a bottle of milk, you could easily walk a mile," commented one analyst.[4]

Walton opened four Hypermarts, but they were not as successful as he had hoped. He ended up closing them all. However, he liked the idea of selling groceries and general merchandise in the same store. He began enlarging some of his Wal-Marts to include a grocery section. He called the new stores "Wal-Mart Supercenters." The new stores were extremely successful.

To many small-town shoppers, Sam Walton was a hero. When other chains ignored them, Walton brought them the same shopping advantages enjoyed by larger communities. But the popularity of Wal-Mart also made it controversial. The company was accused of putting the small mom-and-pop stores out of business. It was blamed for destroying downtown business districts by luring shoppers to their stores on the outskirts of town.

Walton understood their complaints. He had once owned several stores located in rural downtown areas. But times were changing and Walton chose to change with them. He felt that he was helping to improve the lives of small-town residents. He was not forcing shoppers to turn their backs on smaller businesses. He just gave them another option. Most shoppers preferred what the larger stores had to offer.

The notion that Wal-Marts harmed small businesses was confirmed by a study completed in 1989 by Kenneth Stone, an economist from Iowa State University. His research showed that three-fourths of Wal-Mart's sales came at the expense of small businesses.

"[Wal-Mart] moves into town and in the first year they're doing $10 million. That money has to come from somewhere, and generally it's out of the small businessman's cash register," said retail analyst, Jack D. Seibald.[5]

As with most controversies, there were both winners and losers. Towns with a Wal-Mart attracted business from neighboring towns that had no Wal-Mart. This boosted the economy of one town while taking away business from its neighbors.

> **To many small-town shoppers, Sam Walton was a hero.**

Businesses that competed directly with Wal-Mart were often hurt. However, other businesses saw an increase in sales because of the extra people Wal-Mart brought into the area.

Stone encouraged small business owners to change their ways of doing business in order to compete with Wal-Mart. He suggested they sell different items, provide better service, or aim for upscale shoppers.

As the number of discount stores grew, the

Sam Walton campaigns for "buying American" as a solution to the nation's trade deficit problem in 1986.

Pinching Pennies

Sometimes Walton had to get creative to keep his operating expenses low. For several years, he saved on postage by having Wal-Mart trucks carry mail between the Bentonville office and the stores instead of sending it through the U.S. Mail. This was fine except when heavy snowstorms kept trucks from delivering paychecks to the stores. Managers with four-wheel drive vehicles had to battle the icy highways to deliver the checks.

Costs for business trips were kept to a minimum. Fancy hotels and expensive restaurants were unthinkable. Walton insisted that everyone share rooms in modest hotels. Walking was the preferred mode of transportation instead of expensive cabs. Whenever possible, he made appointments early in the morning and late in the evening in order to squeeze more hours of work into each day.

competition among the chains became more intense. Finding goods at the lowest prices possible became even more important. As a result, retailers turned to cheaper products made overseas.

Wal-Mart was not the first company to buy lower-priced merchandise from other countries. By the time Walton began exploring this option, Sears Roebuck, Montgomery Ward, J. C. Penney, and K-Mart were already importing products from Asia. When considering only price, buying overseas made sense. Production costs were much lower because workers were paid very little. But buying products from Asia forced some American factories to close. Many Americans lost their jobs.

In the early 1980s, Walton began looking for ways to bring at least some of those jobs back home. Part of the solution came in 1984 with a call from Arkansas governor, Bill Clinton. The governor told Walton about Ferris Burroughs, a clothing factory in a small Arkansas town. It looked as if the factory would have to close down when its largest customer decided to buy shirts from China instead.

Walton worked with Ferris Burroughs and found that he could buy a large quantity of their shirts for about the same price as the imports. With Wal-Mart as a customer, the factory was able to stay in business.

After successfully helping Ferris Burroughs, Walton started his "Buy American" program to help other companies in the same position. He sent letters to three thousand companies that supplied goods to Wal-Mart and encouraged them to buy more products from U.S. manufacturers. "Our Wal-Mart Company is firmly committed to the philosophy of buying everything possible from suppliers who manufacture their products in the United States," Walton told them.[6]

Wal-Mart's merchandise managers also received a memo from Walton. "Find products that American manufacturers have stopped producing because they couldn't compete with foreign imports."[7]

Walton helped several American companies find ways to compete with the overseas suppliers. In the first year of the Buy American program, Wal-Mart reduced their imports by about 20 percent.

Although Walton cut back on direct imports, that did not tell the whole story. Many of the products Wal-Mart purchased from American companies were made completely or in part in other countries. Even the shirt factory that Walton rescued had to import fabric to make their shirts. Still, Walton's commitment to "Buy American" when possible brought more attention to the problems of importing goods.

In spite of Walton's good intentions, purchases gradually drifted back overseas when American manufacturers could no longer offer the same low prices. The Buy American program ended in 1992, after an embarrassing segment on *Dateline NBC*. Investigative reporters found that, in spite of the signs encouraging shoppers to Buy American, tags on the clothing showed that the garments had been made in Asia.

By 1988, Sam Walton was seventy years old. It was time to start slowing down. He turned over his position as CEO to David Glass. That did not mean that Walton was out of the picture. He still attended Saturday morning meetings and flew around the country visiting stores. He kept up with sales figures and listened to associates share their ideas. As it turned out, turning over the day-to-day running of Wal-Mart to others had been a good idea. Walton soon had a much more serious problem to deal with.

9
GOING OUT IN STYLE

Sam Walton loved hunting, but on one trip he found something he definitely did not want. In November 1989, he was hunting quail on his lease in south Texas. At seventy-one, Walton was still spry, but he was experiencing some odd pains. He had always been a little absentminded, so it was not unusual that he could not find the keys to the icehouse on his hunting lease. Walton noticed an open window, and reached it by climbing onto the shoulders of his dog handler. As Walton squeezed through the window, the dog whistle he was wearing around his neck got caught. It dug painfully into his breastbone. He was still sore the next day, but went hunting anyway. When the pain got worse and spread into his upper arm, Walton decided a trip to his doctor in Houston was called for.

Walton had been making frequent visits to Dr. Quesada at M. D. Anderson Hospital ever since his bout with leukemia seven years earlier. In fact, it had only been three months since his last visit. At that time, Quesada noticed a change in Walton's blood count. Walton was too impatient to stick around a few extra days to find out what caused the change. This time, the doctors tested some of the bone marrow from his hip. Then they broke the bad news to Walton. He had multiple myeloma—cancer of the bone marrow. The disease was incurable and aggressive. The interferon Walton had used for his leukemia would not work this time. Quesada recommended chemotherapy and radiation treatments in hopes of sending the disease into remission.

Back at home, Walton studied to learn as much as he could about cancer treatments. He even looked at ones that were experimental or out of the range of normal medicine. Finally, he gave up and agreed to undergo the treatment plan Quesada had recommended. Deep down he knew that in all likelihood, he would not survive this bout with cancer.[1]

As before, Walton felt the need to share his diagnosis with his associates—now numbering 250,000. His heartfelt message was sent over the Wal-Mart telecommunication network. After mentioning his successful treatment for leukemia seven years earlier, Walton broke the latest news. "Last week, I was informed that I have contracted another form of cancer called Multiple Myeloma, a bone disease; and that has apparently accounted for my many aches and pains these past 60 to 90 days."[2]

Walton kept the message upbeat. He told his associates that he had started chemotherapy and was already feeling better. He added that he hoped to start visiting stores again soon.

At the time Walton learned that he had cancer, he was working on an autobiography with Eric Morgenthaler, a reporter with the *Wall Street Journal.* Walton was a very private man. He disliked sitting around trying to think about his past. He told Morgenthaler that after his cancer diagnosis, he wanted to simplify his life and get rid of the things he did not want to do. Writing an autobiography was one of them. The book had not been Walton's idea anyway. He was talked into it by his family and some of the Wal-Mart executives.

Later, as the cancer progressed, his family and coworkers again suggested that he write his autobiography. This time he chose John Huey, a reporter with *Fortune,* to help him. *Sam Walton: Made in America* was released soon after Walton's death. His share of the record $4 million book advance and royalties was donated to an educational charity.

During his illness, Walton saw Wal-Mart reach two milestones. In November 1990, it passed up

K-Mart to become the second largest retailer in the United States. A few months later, Wal-Mart's $32.7 billion in sales moved it ahead of Sears Roebuck to become the nation's largest retailer.

Even more exciting news came to the Walton household. President George H. W. Bush was coming to Bentonville to present Walton with the Presidential Medal of Freedom. This award is the highest honor the government can give to a civilian.

It was not hard for Walton to decide who to invite to the ceremony. On March 17, 1992, the Wal-Mart

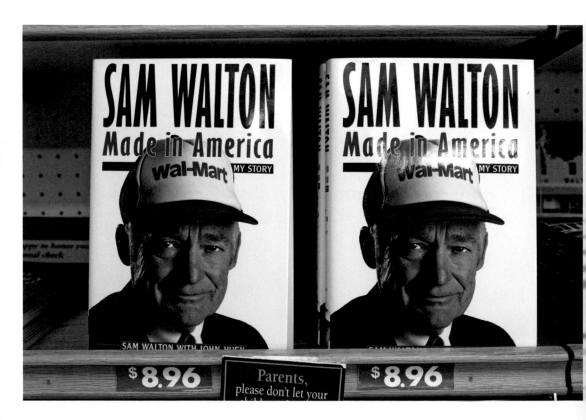

Sam Walton's autobiography, *Sam Walton: Made in America*, would be released shortly after Walton's death in 1992.

auditorium was packed with hundreds of associates and friends. It might have seemed like a Saturday morning meeting if it were not for President and Mrs. Bush on stage. The room rang with an exuberant Wal-Mart cheer. Walton was pushed onto the stage in a wheelchair, his body too frail to make the walk himself.

President Bush praised Walton for his hard work, his small-town values, his determination to follow his dream, and the ambition to make it come true. "His nation honors him today as the outstanding example of American initiative and achievement. And at the same time, we take note that as he became more and more successful he never turned his back on his roots," said the president. He went on to praise Walton for living a lifestyle that "kept him close to his family, his friends, and his community."[3]

As President Bush neared the end of his speech, his voice was choked with emotion. "I salute you, sir, for your vision, and I am proud to give you your nation's highest civilian honor."[4]

Walton slowly rose from his wheelchair and stood proudly as Helen Walton fastened the Medal of Freedom around her husband's neck. The room erupted in boisterous cheers and applause.

After thanking the president, Walton praised all the Wal-Mart employees. "We're proud of what we have accomplished. We think we have just begun," he said. Then he added, "This is the highlight of my career." [5]

Only a few days after receiving the Medal of Freedom, Walton entered the University of Arkansas hospital in Little Rock. He continued to keep his spirits up and enjoyed having company. One of his last visitors was the manager of a Wal-Mart in Little Rock. He and Walton went over the latest sales figures for his store.

Sam Walton stands alongside President George H. W. Bush in Bentonville, Arkansas, on March 18, 1992, shortly after being awarded the Medal of Freedom.

Sam Walton died on April 5, 1992, just days after his seventy-fourth birthday and nineteen days after receiving the Medal of Freedom. His memorial service was broadcast over the satellite system to Wal-Mart associates across the country.

It is unusual for one man to revolutionize an entire industry, but that is exactly what Sam Walton did. He transformed the shopping habits of a nation, and in doing so, changed the small towns themselves.

In the end, it was Walton's personality that endeared him to millions. "Mr. Sam" was a giant who was humble. Throughout his life, he held firm to his values of hard work, thriftiness, modesty, and respect for others. He insisted on first-class treatment for everyone in his stores, from his loyal associates to his customers.

What would Wal-Mart do without him?

Sharing the Wealth

Hundreds of causes receive support from the Waltons. In 1987, the Walton Family Foundation was formed to manage the family's charitable donations. Since the Walton's are private people, most of their giving is done with little or no publicity. Education is their strongest interest because it impacts so many areas of society. Between 1998 and early 2004, the foundation donated over $700 million to educational charities.[6] The Waltons have also donated millions of dollars to help construct buildings, such as the Walton Arts Center near the University of Arkansas, and a fine arts center at the University of the Ozarks in Clarksville, Arkansas. In 2003, the family donated a $300 million matching grant to the University of Arkansas to be used for an honors college and graduate programs.

10
WAL-MART WITHOUT WALTON

Sam Walton was gone. For the first time, Wal-Mart faced the future without the man who was not only its creator, but was its heart and soul. Business analysts wondered if the retail giant could keep up the momentum without its leader. "He was such a central figure. He was Wal-Mart," said Kent Marts, editor of the *Benton County Daily Record*.[1]

Long before his death, Walton had put in place a leadership team with people who shared his philosophy. In 1988, he had promoted David Glass to president and CEO. Rob Walton replaced his father as chairman of Wal-Mart. This assured that someone from the family was in a key position without actually running the company. The Walton family remains influential as Wal-Mart's largest stockholder.

Walton laid the groundwork for the Wal-Mart empire, but Glass is credited with leading the company's aggressive growth in the 1990s. He had been schooled in the Wal-Mart culture, but he and Walton differed in many respects. Walton was cautious about spending money. He worried about Wal-Mart getting too big. "I always wanted to be the best retailer in the world, not necessarily the biggest. I've always been a little bit afraid that big might get in the way of doing a good job," Walton once said.[2]

Glass had no fear of growth or increased debt. He borrowed money to pay for expansion, but his strongest contribution was improving technology. "A long time ago I had a strong belief that technology would ultimately drive this business to be the size that it is," said Glass.[3]

His aggressive strategy worked. In the three years following Walton's death, Wal-Mart sales nearly doubled to almost $100 billion. *Fortune* called it "an unmatched feat in the annals of the *Fortune 500*."[4] By early 2002, Wal-Mart's $218 billion in sales made it the largest corporation in the world.

Two things spurred Wal-Mart's explosive growth— Supercenters and overseas expansion. Supercenters began slowly in 1988. By August 1994, the number of larger stores had grown to one hundred. Eight years later, that number had jumped to 1,060. Adding grocery stores to traditional Wal-Marts often doubled the store's profit. By 2001, Wal-Mart had become America's leading grocer.

Wal-Mart also expanded by opening stores in other countries. This trend began in the early 1990s with the first store in Mexico City. By the end of 2005, Wal-Mart was operating 1,732 stores in nine countries.

Sam Walton's spirit is visible even in the international stores. Associates speak different languages, but there are still greeters at the doors and enthusiastic workers shouting the Wal-Mart cheer. Walton's photographs and quotations still hang on the walls for

Today, the "Wal-Mart cheer" continues as a daily routine in many Wal-Mart stores. Here, the manager of the Bentonville Wal-Mart leads employees in the cheer on March 16, 2005.

Where Are They Now?

When Sam Walton died, he left behind his wife, four children, and 39 percent of Wal-Mart's stock. What were the members of America's richest family doing in 2005?

Walton's widow, Helen, still lived in the family home in Bentonville. At eighty-six, her activities had been limited by injuries received in an automobile accident in 1999. She remains very interested in the family business.[5]

Eldest son, Rob Walton, took his father's place as chairman of Wal-Mart. He is the most involved in the business and serves as the link between the family and the company. He frequently pilots his own plane between Bentonville and his home in Arizona.

John Walton, who decades earlier had received a Silver Star for saving lives under fire in Vietnam, was tragically killed on June 27, 2005. The ultralight plane he was piloting crashed soon after takeoff from Jackson Hole, Wyoming. Before his death, John sat on the board of the Walton Family Foundation, which manages the family's charitable contributions, many of which go to improving education.

Jim Walton, who also sits on the Wal-Mart Board of Directors, manages the Walton's family owned businesses. This includes Walton Enterprises, which holds the family's Wal-Mart stock, as well as the banks and newspapers owned by the Waltons.

Alice Walton once owned her own investment company. She has been influential in economic and quality-of-life improvements in northwestern Arkansas. She worked hard to get an airport built in Wal-Mart's hometown of Bentonville, as well as improved highways for the area. One recent priority project in northwestern Arkansas was building Camp War Eagle for children of all races and economic levels. The Walton Foundation provides scholarships for underprivileged children to attend. Alice was also influential in bringing a world-class art museum and cultural center to Bentonville.

inspiration. Associates are still trained to put customers first, and every day low prices remain a top priority.

Much of Wal-Mart International's focus is on China, whose 1.3 billion people offer a great potential for growth. The first Wal-Mart Supercenter opened in Shenzhen in August 1996. More than eighty thousand shoppers crowded into the store the first day. Wal-Mart's packaged foods, clean floors, and wide aisles were a vast improvement over the open-air "wet markets" the customers were used to. The store was stocked with Chinese favorites such as live fish, eels, snakes, frogs, and sea cucumbers.

As Wal-Mart's size increased, so did the controversies surrounding the company. Most of the arguments had been around a long time. Wal-Mart was still accused of hurting small businesses, paying low wages, and being anti-union.

"Some of what they are saying is right. And it hurts to be vilified," Rob Walton admitted. "But some of our opponents have agendas too. The unions are looking to organize. When you are the biggest company in the world you get this kind of attention."[6]

Whether or not Wal-Mart is good or bad for America depends on whom you talk to. Wal-Mart is considered by many to be the most efficiently run large company in the country. As a result, they are able to sell merchandise for prices lower than their competitors. This helps hold down the cost of living for the

138 million customers who shop in Wal-Marts each week.

On the other side, there are many people who think that Wal-Mart is bad for America. These include labor unions that have been unable to unionize Wal-Mart employees. It includes workers who lost their jobs when their companies moved overseas to save expenses. And it includes many people who worry about Wal-Mart's effect on national and world economies.

Does Wal-Mart hurt the communities it moves into? While stores competing head-to-head with Wal-Mart often fail, the community's overall economy usually benefits. A study conducted at Ryerson University in 2002 found that when Wal-Mart moves into an area, local sales increase and many new stores are added.[7] Businesses located near Wal-Marts usually flourish.

Wal-Mart's effect on America's overall economy is not as clear. On the plus side, Wal-Mart has been credited with lowering the cost of living, even for those who do not shop there. A recent economic study by an independent firm, Global Insight, found that Wal-Mart saves the average U.S. household more than $2,300 annually. Its competitors have been forced to find more efficient ways of doing business in order to lower their own prices. This has slowed the rate of inflation and improved the standard of living for the poor. "If you're stuck with a low income and you can reduce the amount you pay for basic items, then your real income goes up," said economist Bruce Bartlett.[8]

Unfortunately, there is a downside to Wal-Mart's low prices. "If a company achieves its lower prices by finding better and smarter ways of doing things, then yes, everybody wins," said *Fortune* reporter Jerry Useem. "But if it cuts costs by cutting pay and benefits—or by sending production to China—then not everybody wins."[9]

Every time an American company closes or moves to China, its workers lose their jobs. Many of those workers have trouble finding new jobs or must settle for ones that pay much less. This not only affects the workers and their families, it affects the economy of their communities as well.

"Wal-Mart certainly does lower the cost of living for American consumers by offering low prices, but it also lowers the standard of living, because as jobs leave the U.S., the country's wage level gets lowered, too," explained Alan Tonelson, from the United States Business and Industry Council.[10]

Low wages are a key issue in the ongoing clash between Wal-Mart and labor unions. This battle is especially visible in California. Grocery stores staffed by union workers have a hard time competing with Wal-Mart Supercenters, whose groceries are 17 to 39 percent cheaper, according to one study.[11] Unionized

A portrait of Sam Walton is unveiled by artist Mike Wimmer on the floor of the state Senate in Oklahoma City, Oklahoma, in March 2005.

grocery workers earn an average of $10 more per hour in wages and benefits than do Wal-Mart workers.[12] The only way their stores can compete is to cut back on employee benefits, such as health care.

Wal-Mart has retained Walton's steadfast opposition to unions. They point out that many more people apply for jobs than there are openings, proving that people want to work for Wal-Mart. The company downplays the fact that having unionized workers would increase Wal-Mart's operating costs, hurting its ability to keep prices low.

Unions are getting desperate. Stuart Acuff, organizing director of the AFL-CIO, told *Fortune,* "If we want to survive, [labor] has no choice but to organize Wal-Mart."[13]

As a result, the unions have changed their tactics. They use lawsuits, zoning fights, and negative publicity to discredit Wal-Mart in order to slow down its growth. "It's an effort to destroy Wal-Mart because the company's continued growth and success is really an argument against the need for unionization," said Elisa Sumanski, a legal analyst with the National Right to Work Legal Defense Foundation.[14]

Emotions run high on both sides in the battle between Wal-Mart and unions. Reaching a satisfactory outcome seems nearly impossible at this time.

Being the world's largest corporation gives Wal-Mart a lot of power. Manufacturers that cannot meet Wal-Mart's terms are not likely to see their products on Wal-Mart shelves. This has forced many of them to move overseas in order to compete

"They control so much of retail that they can put someone into business or take someone out of business if they choose to," said Pat Danahy, with Cone Mills Corp., one of the few surviving U.S. textile producers.[15]

In spite of its controversies, Wal-Mart continues to be highly respected in the business community. In 1999, *Discount Store News* made Wal-Mart its "Retailer of the Century." In 2003 and 2004, *Fortune* named

Wal-Mart as America's Most Admired Company, as chosen by a poll of ten thousand executives, directors, and analysts. The award was especially impressive in 2003, when Wal-Mart became the first company in the magazine's history to top the *Fortune 500* and the *Most Admired Company* lists in the same year. Under the leadership of Lee Scott, who replaced David Glass as CEO in 2000, Wal-Mart is expected to keep growing and improving.

It is no secret that Wal-Mart has detractors, but most communities appreciate their presence. Wal-Mart makes an effort to be a good corporate neighbor by giving back to their local communities. In 2004, they

A Wal-Mart employee at work in Shanghai, China, in July 2005.

matched $61 million in grants to support community groups, such as schools, youth programs, fire departments, libraries, hospitals, and other organizations. The company gave out $6 million in college scholarships to six thousand high-school seniors.

Wal-Mart is quick to respond when their communities are hit by natural disasters. When Hurricane Katrina devastated the Gulf Coast during the summer of 2005, Wal-Mart donated $18 million in cash to the relief effort. They also gave much needed supplies to command centers and shelters in the affected areas. Associates who had to flee to other areas were given assistance and jobs in their new locations.

Wal-Mart began with one unimpressive store selling a hodgepodge of products and grew to be the largest company in the world. It succeeded because Sam Walton kept dreaming bigger dreams and nourished them with hard work and down-home values.

If Walton could see his company today, he would probably not be completely surprised. He once said, "I had no vision of the scope of what I would start, but I always had confidence that as long as we did our work well, and were good to our customers, there would be no limit to us."[16]

CHRONOLOGY

1918   Samuel Moore Walton is born in Kingfisher, Oklahoma, on March 29.

1936   Walton graduates from Hickman High School, Columbia, Missouri.

1940   Walton graduates from the University of Missouri with a degree in economics and begins work at a J. C. Penney store in Des Moines, Iowa.

1942   Walton works at a gunpowder plant in Pryor, Oklahoma, before being drafted into the army. He meets his future wife, Helen Robson.

1943   Sam Walton and Helen Robson are married on February 14.

1944   The Waltons' first son, Samuel Robson Walton ("Rob"), is born.

1945   Upon leaving the army, Walton opens his first Ben Franklin variety store in Newport, Arkansas.

1946   Second son, John Thomas Walton, is born.

1948   Third son, James Carr Walton, is born.

Daughter, Alice Walton, is born.	**1949**
Walton loses his Newport store when landlord refuses to renew his lease. The family moves to Bentonville, Arkansas, where he opens WALTON'S 5¢-10¢.	**1950**
Walton buys a second store in Fayetteville, Arkansas, and makes it self-service.	**1952**
Sam and Bud Walton open a variety store in a shopping center near Kansas City, Missouri.	**1954**
Walton opens the first Wal-Mart in Rogers, Arkansas.	**1962**
Wal-Mart stock is offered to the public for the first time. Wal-Mart opens its first distribution center and headquarters in Bentonville.	**1970**
Walton temporarily retires and names Ron Mayer as CEO.	**1974**
Walton reclaims the leadership of Wal-Mart, ending his twenty-month retirement.	**1976**
Wal-Mart reaches $1 billion in sales.	**1979**
Walton is diagnosed with hairy-cell leukemia.	**1982**
The first Sam's Warehouse Club opens near Oklahoma City.	**1983**

1984   Walton dances the hula on Wall Street in
New York City after losing a bet concerning
company profits.

1985   Walton is named *Forbes* magazine's Richest
Man in America with a net worth estimated
at $2.8 billion. Walton introduces his "Buy
American" program.

1987   Wal-Mart completes construction of the
largest private satellite communications
system in the United States.

1988   Walton appoints David Glass as CEO of
Wal-Mart. The first Wal-Mart Supercenter
opens in Washington, Missouri.

1989   Walton is diagnosed with bone cancer.

1991   Wal-Mart becomes the largest retailer in
the nation by earning more than both
K-mart and Sears.

1992   President George H. W. Bush honors Walton
with the Presidential Medal of Freedom.
Walton dies on April 5, just nineteen days
after receiving his medal.

CHAPTER NOTES

Chapter 1. Gambling on Life

1. Vance H. Trimble, *Sam Walton: The Inside Story of America's Richest Man* (New York: Dutton, 1990), p. 201.

2. Bob Ortega, *In Sam We Trust: The Untold Story of Sam Walton and How Wal-Mart Is Devouring America* (New York: Random House, 1998), p. 6.

3. Ibid., p. 6.

Chapter 2. The Boy From Kingfisher

1. Sam Walton with John Huey, *Sam Walton: Made in America* (New York: Doubleday, 1992), p. 4.

2. Bob Ortega, *In Sam We Trust: The Untold Story of Sam Walton and How Wal-Mart Is Devouring America* (New York: Random House, 1998), p. 20.

3. Walton and Huey, p. 11.

4. Vance H. Trimble, *Sam Walton: The Inside Story of America's Richest Man* (New York: Dutton, 1990), p. 26.

Chapter 3. Not Cut Out for Retail?

1. Sam Walton with John Huey, *Sam Walton: Made in America* (New York: Doubleday, 1992), p. 18.

2. Vance H. Trimble, *Sam Walton: The Inside Story of America's Richest Man* (New York: Dutton, 1990), pp. 34–35.

3. "Sam Walton: Bargain Billionaire," *A&E Biography*, Cat. No. AAE-14274, December 2, 1997 (videocassette).

4. "A Willingness to Fail Proves Key to Success," *Chain Store Age*, December 1999, p. 6.

5. Ibid.

6. Walton and Huey, p. 6.

7. "Life of a Salesman," *TIME*, June 15, 1992, p. 52.

8. Walton and Huey, p. 22.

9. Richard S. Tedlow, "Sam Walton: Great From the Start," *Harvard Business School: Working Knowledge*, July 23, 2001.

10. Ibid.

11. Walton and Huey, p. 30.

Chapter 4. Starting Over

1. Richard S. Tedlow, "Sam Walton: Great From the Start," *Harvard Business School: Working Knowledge*, July 23, 2001.

2. Sam Walton with John Huey, *Sam Walton: Made in America* (New York: Doubleday, 1992), p. 40.

3. Vance H. Trimble, *Sam Walton: The Inside Story of America's Richest Man* (New York: Dutton, 1990), p. 75.

4. Ibid., pp. 75–76.

5. Sandra S. Vance and Roy V. Scott, *Wal-Mart: A History of Sam Walton's Retail Phenomenon* (New York: Twayne Publishers, 1994), p. 43.

Chapter 5. Birth of a Giant

1. Sandra S. Vance and Roy V. Scott, *Wal-Mart: A*

History of Sam Walton's Retail Phenomenon (New York: Twayne Publishers, 1994), p. 41.

2. Ibid., p. 43.

3. Ibid., p. 45.

4. Vance H. Trimble, *Sam Walton: The Inside Story of America's Richest Man* (New York: Dutton, 1990), p. 4.

5. Arthur Markowitz, "Mr. Sam: Wal-Mart's Patriarch," *Discount Store News,* December 18, 1989.

6. Ibid.

7. Bob Ortega, *In Sam We Trust: The Untold Story of Sam Walton and How Wal-Mart Is Devouring America* (New York: Random House, 1998), p. 59.

8. "Life of a Salesman," *TIME,* June 15, 1992, p. 52.

9. Sam Walton with John Huey, *Sam Walton: Made in America* (New York: Doubleday, 1992), p. 112.

10. Vance and Scott, p. 51.

11. Ortega, p. 66.

12. Vance and Scott, p. 51.

Chapter 6. Going Public

1. Vance H. Trimble, *Sam Walton: The Inside Story of America's Richest Man* (New York: Dutton, 1990), p. 130.

2. Sam Walton with John Huey, *Sam Walton: Made in America* (New York: Doubleday, 1992), p. 99.

3. Bob Ortega, *In Sam We Trust: The Untold Story of Sam Walton and How Wal-Mart Is Devouring America* (New York: Random House, 1998), p. 209.

4. Jay L. Johnson, "Wal-Mart's Secret Weapon," *Discount Merchandiser,* August 1993, p. 66.

5. Walton and Huey, p. 130.

6. Ibid., p. 165.

7. Trimble, p. 173.

8. Don Soderquist, *The Wal-Mart Way* (Nashville, Tenn.: Nelson Business, 2005), p. 23.

9. Walton and Huey, p. 196.

10. M. Loeb, "A Rare Look at Sam Walton," *Fortune*, June 29, 1992, p. 4.

Chapter 7. Tackling the Competition

1. Bob Ortega, *In Sam We Trust: The Untold Story of Sam Walton and How Wal-Mart Is Devouring America* (New York: Random House, 1998), p. 107.

2. Ibid., p. 230.

3. Sandra S. Vance and Roy V. Scott, *Wal-Mart: A History of Sam Walton's Retail Phenomenon* (New York: Twayne Publishers, 1994), p. 93.

4. Ortega, p. 147.

5. Ibid., p. 142.

6. Jim Collins, "The 10 Greatest CEOs of All Time," *Fortune*, July 21, 2003.

7. Vance H. Trimble, *Sam Walton: The Inside Story of America's Richest Man* (New York: Dutton, 1990), p. 211.

8. Corey Hajim, "Sam Walton Explores the Final Frontier," *Fortune*, June 27, 2005, p. 82.

Chapter 8. Growing Pains

1. Howard Rudnitsky, "Play it Again, Sam," *Forbes*, August 10, 1987, p. 48.

2. Sam Walton with John Huey, *Sam Walton: Made in America* (New York: Doubleday, 1992), p. 3.

3. Sandra S. Vance and Roy V. Scott, *Wal-Mart: A*

History of Sam Walton's Retail Phenomenon (New York: Twayne Publishers, 1994), p. 98.

4. Walton and Huey, p. 112.

5. "Sam Walton." *Business Leader Profiles for Students,* Vol. 1, Gale Research, 1999, p. 814.

6. Bob Ortega, *In Sam We Trust: The Untold Story of Sam Walton and How Wal-Mart Is Devouring America* (New York: Random House, 1998), p. 204.

7. Lee Laughlin, "Wal-Mart Buys $197M Worth of U.S. Goods," *Daily News Record,* May 23, 1986, p. 4.

Chapter 9 Going Out in Style

1. Sam Walton with John Huey, *Sam Walton: Made in America* (New York: Doubleday, 1992), p. 258.

2. Bob Ortega, *In Sam We Trust: The Untold Story of Sam Walton and How Wal-Mart Is Devouring America* (New York: Random House, 1998), p. 219.

3. Jay L. Johnson, "Wal-Mart's Secret Weapon," Discount Merchandiser, August 1993, p. 66.

4. "Medal of Freedom," Wal-Martstores.com VideoLibrary,<http://walmart.feedroom.com/ifr_main.jsp?nsid=b271e7063:10e112800da:5db6&st=1159932102173&mp=FLV&cpf=false&fvn=8&fr=100306_112141_271e7063x10e112800dax5db7&rdm=319249.67389518843> (April 21, 2006).

5. Ibid.

6. Jim Hopkins, "Wal-Mart Heirs Pour Riches Into Reforming Education," *USA Today,* March 11, 2004.

Chapter 10. Wal-Mart Without Walton

1. Robert Slater, *The Wal-Mart Decade* (New York: Portfolio, 2003), p. 72.

2. Ibid., p. 92.

3. Ibid., p. 87.

4. Jerry Useem, "Should We Admire Wal-Mart?" *Fortune,* March 8, 2004.

5. Andy Serwer, "The Waltons: Inside America's Richest Family," *Fortune,* November 15, 2004, pp. 86–116.

6. Ibid.

7. Steve Maich, "Why Wal-Mart Is Good," *Maclean's,* July 25, 2005, p. 26.

8. Ibid.

9. Useem.

10. "Is Wal-Mart Good for America?—interview, Alan Tonelson" *Frontline,* PBS, May 27, 2004, <http://www.pbs.org/wgbh/pages/frontline/shows/wal-mart/interviews/tonelson.html> (April 14, 2006).

11. Nancy Cleeland and Abigail Goldman, "An Empire Built on Bargains Remakes the Working World," *Los Angeles Times,* November 23, 2003.

12. Ibid.

13. Maich, p. 7.

14. Ibid., p. 8.

15. Cleeland and Goldman.

16. Don Soderquist, *The Wal-Mart Way* (Nashville, Tenn.: Nelson Business, 2005), p. 6.

FURTHER READING

Books

Dougherty, Terri. *Sam Walton: Department Store Giant.* Farmington Hills, Mich.: Blackbirch Press, 2004.

Mavis, B. *Sam Walton.* Langhorn, Penn.: Chelsea House, 1995.

Walton, Sam, with John Huey. *Sam Walton: Made in America.* New York: Doubleday, 1992.

Video

"Sam Walton: Bargain Billionaire," *A&E, Biography,* Cat. # AAE-14274, December 2, 1997.

Internet Addresses

"Is Wal-Mart Good for America?"
<http://www.pbs.org/wgbh/pages/frontline/shows/walmart>

Wal-Mart Online Visitor's Center
<http://www.walmartstores.com/Files/MainMenu.html>

INDEX